STOP, PRAY, LISTEN, OBEY

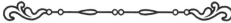

A Thirty-Three-Day
Devotional Journey that will
Bring Inspiration!

Tammy McKie

ISBN 978-1-64569-854-8 (paperback)
ISBN 978-1-64569-855-5 (digital)

Christian Faith Publishing, Inc.
832 Park Avenue
Meadville, PA 16335
www.christianfaithpublishing.com

Printed in the United States of America

Introduction

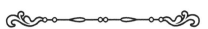

I am a human being who does human things in a body that God made. I lived most of my life not really understanding what it meant to be made by God. I knew about God, I went to church some growing up, but all of those Bible stories really seemed a bit far-fetched to me, and down deep, I was a person full of fear and anxiety.

I always heard "God is love," but I really never understood though what that actually looked like in people, and it was hard for me to imagine that if God *was* love, why all the "bad" in the world? I knew we went to heaven when we died (if we were *good enough*, so I thought), but still in the back of my mind, I had concerns, and I don't think I truly believed it in my heart.

I looked back now on all of the times God was chasing me. My most fond memory is at a church camp when I was seventeen, and I was dunked in a pool of water and baptized. I was on fire for Jesus for about five minutes. (Ha!) Then I drew away from chasing after Him for the most part because of the *behavior* I saw in "church folk." So much judgment and pride and "holier than thou" on the outside. I certainly didn't see much *love* going on inside most of the churches that I attended.

I threw myself into church volunteerism for most of my adult life. I thought it was the thing to do and a good idea to raise my children in a church, learning about Jesus. It was a *great* idea; however, it was still very puzzling to me that if God was all about *love* and *peace*, why was I still feeling so much fear and anxiety? I would read in the Bible that God brought a "peace that surpasses all understanding" and that "the Joy of the Lord was my strength" and "I could do all things through Christ that gives me strength" and "He has a plan to prosper me and not to harm me" and "all things are possible with God" and "He did not give me a spirit of fear or timidity, but one of power, love and a sound mind." But, But…there was still this unbelief and worrisome nature that I know *now* was actually the *enemy* (Satan, the devil, the liar, the inner critic, the accuser) keeping me from truly believing the scriptures and actually pulling me away from the purpose and life that God had for me.

It wasn't until a dozen or so years ago when I was drawn (I know *now* by the Holy Spirit) to have a one-on-one time with the Bible and God, that my life *changed*. I mean, really *changed*…my stinkin' thinkin' was replaced by this beautiful Word of God that my eyes were not open to until I got into it *myself*. Oh, it was hard at first, even sitting down for five minutes to do a little reading of the Word and *pray*. My mind would just start to wander, so I began to *write down* my prayers.

This "alone time with God" turned into something I could *not* get enough of! I started seeing prayers answered, and scriptures coming to *life*! My fears and anxieties became less and less, and then I started seeing God in *everything*. I would actually practice "listening" to what I thought God was saying to me or showing me, and again, *it changed my life* to the better. I began to live *supernaturally*, naturally. :-)

God wants to guide us. He wants to give us blessing after blessing and show us our *purpose, but,* we must be *obedient* to His promptings. They are everywhere! :-)

Whenever you start feeling *anything* or acting out *anything* that is *not* of God, you must capture those thoughts and *stop* that thinking or doing. Then you *pray* about it. Then you *listen* to what you think the Holy Spirit is saying. Then you *obey*.

I pray that this devotional journey helps you to understand who you are in God and that when you *stop, pray, listen, obey,* your life will be so enriched by His *power* that He so freely gives us through His *grace*.

Jesus said, after all, *greater* things shall *we* do! :-)

With love,
Tammy

DAY 1

Be still, and know that I am God.

—Psalms 46:10

It was a tough start for me. I didn't think I had five minutes to spare in the mornings as I got myself ready for work and my children ready for their day. And the suggestion of getting *up* a little earlier?! Uh, *no*, I enjoyed my sleep too much. However, *something* inside of me was *drawing* me to do this, so I began to get up ten minutes early each morning and would sit at my breakfast table with my devotional book and my Bible. I would read the scripture from the devotional and ask God to help me understand it. I would then read the devotional that went with it, and then I would pray. Well, I would *try* to pray. My mind would start to wander about various things. Mostly to my "plans" for that day: what was I going to wear for work that day, what was I was going to put in my son's lunch, how was I going to handle this problem at work, etc. Ugh, *every* time, my mind would wander! I had heard a couple of people talk about journaling their prayers, so I decided to try that.

What a revelation! It was awesome. I became quite good at journaling and writing down what was in my heart. I was not just petitioning for what I needed. I found myself starting to *thank Him* over and over in my prayers. I began to see people's faces and pray for them. I would get a holy anger at times and tell God what I was mad about, and I, of course, asked for forgiveness for myself and others, and I did a little confessing. (I'm human, remember?) :-)

5

I go back and look through some of those journals every once in a while, and I am blown away with how many of my prayers got *results*. I knew it was because I was taking the time to listen for what I felt *God* wanted me to pray for. It wasn't all about *me* and my wants and needs and self-pity.

It takes practice to be still before the Lord and give Him your undivided attention. Oh, but it will be so worth it. I promise…well, He promises.

Thought for the Day: God has something to say, and we need to be still with Him and take the time to listen if we want a life full of *love* and *joy*, and a *peace* that surpasses all understanding.

DAY 2

They (believers) shall lay hands on the sick, and they shall recover.
—Mark 16:18

N ow this one I was ready to test! I considered myself a believer, but still wasn't completely sold on healing. It was *Jesus* that told us "lay your hands on the sick and they will recover," per the writings of Mark. He told us we could do a lot of other cool stuff as believers too—you should read the whole chapter.

My family and myself had suffered a lot of illness up to this point. I thought, *Wow, so many other families of whom I thought were believers have suffered illness too, why do we not hear of a lot more supernatural healings?* This was the point I decided to put my faith to the test. It really boils down to the individual faith that we have in Jesus telling us to do these things.

At the time, my son was about nine years old. His legs were covered in warts, and he was so embarrassed about it that he would not wear shorts. I decided that I was going to lay my hands on those nasty warts, and they were going to *disappear*. My son was all for it. I explained to him that the Bible said we could heal him, and he was ready for it. At bedtime that night, I laid my hands on his legs, and we prayed for the virus to go away in Jesus's name.

He got up the next morning still covered in warts and said in a really sad voice, "It didn't work, Mom," and I told him we would try again that night. I asked him, "Do you believe that God can heal your warts?," and he quickly said, "*Yes!*" So we tried again that night. Then the next morning, no change. I told him that I still believed

7

God's Word, and I thought we ought to try it again. We tried a third night. At this point, we thought, *Why not?*

The next morning was a Saturday. We had nothing going on this particular morning, so my husband and I were just lying there enjoying the quiet before the kids got up. Fairly early, not giving my husband and I time to rest, my son came running into my husband's and my bedroom. He was screaming, "They're gone! They're gone! They're gone!" It took me a moment to get out of my sleepy trance to know what he has talking about. We were amazed! Every single place where a wart had been on his body was a flat white circle of skin. Praise God! Not to mention, it was a bonus that my husband happened to still be in bed that morning to rejoice with us. My husband got tears in his eyes. An increase in faith surely had occurred for not just me and my son. As a bonus, those pesky white spots were gone the next day, and my son was fully healed! No warts ever returned!

I encourage you to listen to your inner voice, the Holy Spirit, when it comes to laying your hands on the sick. I have discovered that if God reveals it, He will heal it! There is a time for everything. I have found that sometimes, if the person does not heal, it is not time for the recovery. We have to trust God. If we have been obedient and laid our hands on the sick like His Word says, then we've done our part, and the rest is up to God.

Thought for the Day: Sickness does not come from God. He wants to use our vessels to send His healing power into the earth. Be obedient to the scripture and do what it tells you to do. Then just trust God. It is never *our* power that does the healing. It will always be God's power. Then we will be rewarded for our obedience.

DAY 3

And be not conformed to this world: but be ye transformed
by the renewing of your mind, that ye may prove what is
that good, and acceptable, and perfect, will of God.

—Mark 16:18

This is a *big*, important one. We must practice renewing our mind *daily*. The enemy, that inner critic, is constantly trying to get our minds on what is *not* of God and on what is usually harmful for us. "Stinkin' thinkin'" is what I like to call it. Our minds are the enemy's biggest playground. We must not give him control of our thoughts!

This brings me to the thoughts of one day when I was at a Bible study meeting and heard, "Everything you read, everything you watch, everything you hear, must be about God right now." My first reaction was, *No way, I am not going to turn into some religious freak who won't read a romance novel or watch an R-rated movie, or listen to some good ol' country music!* Then God showed me exactly what was happening to me.

Every time I'd read a romance novel, my thoughts would go to, *I wish my husband loved me like that, I wish my husband would compliment me like that,* or *he should make me feel like the most beautiful person in the world.* When I'd hear a country song, my thoughts would go to, *Oh, I wish I could go out country dancing, my husband won't dance with me...he's so mean,* and on and on. That is some "stinkin' thinkin'" right there. It would send me into a world of self-pity and make me feel so resentful. *That is not of God.*

This drove me into a new season of my new Christian life. I had to build up my spirit with everything of God so that when the stinkin' thinkin' came, I could capture those thoughts and cast them down. I began to listen to Christian songs. The songs helped me to learn more scripture and use it as a weapon against the thoughts the enemy would try to put in my head.

Okay, I'm not saying that you can never watch, read, or listen to anything other than Christian stuff. What I am saying is that when you are starting your close walk with the Lord, it is a good idea to fill your spirit up with *only Him* so that you have the ability to *fight and win* the spiritual battles and thoughts that the enemy is going to most assuredly try to place on you and in you. We must get *prepared* for that battle; otherwise, we will be constantly opening the door up to emotions and behaviors that could harm us.

Thought for the Day: Tune into the church channel while getting ready for the day, crank up the Christian station in the car, read the Bible. The Lord has some things to say to us through those avenues, and we will build up our spirit!

DAY 4

(As it is written, I have made thee a father of many nations) before
him whom he believed, even God, who quickeneth the dead,
and calleth those things which be not as though they were.

—Romans 4:17

There are many scriptures regarding the power that our spoken words have. We can choose to speak "life" or "death." We can create things with our words because we are made of God's image, and God *spoke* everything into existence. Our thoughts can even open a door for the enemy to get in and for things to take place that we don't want!

This particular scripture in Romans has come to life for my family in many instances, but this one stands out the most to me. I always told my daughter to "speak things that are not as though they were" because our words are *so* powerful. One of my favorite testimonies of this was with her. She was seventeen years old and a carhop at Sonic Drive-In. She was getting ready to go into work one cold, rainy evening, and she was not feeling well. She came to me in tears saying things like, "This night is going to be miserable" and "I haven't even made enough money recently for this job to be worth it." Of course, I did our "family thing" and said, "Oh no, no, no, don't speak that out!" After she did a bit of eye-rolling (teenagers, ha!), I grabbed her hands and prayed, "God, give her the best night of her Sonic career. She's going to get the biggest tip she has ever received." My daughter finally wiped her tears, grinned, and said it in agreement with me.

She had to close that night, so it was about eleven when she got home. Despite the late hours, she ran into my room and showed me a $50 bill a single customer had given to her at Sonic that night. At Sonic, you know…where the most expensive meal is around $5. I am not one for math, but I think that is like a 10,000 percent tip. We rejoiced and got so tickled! She said that the woman only bought a soda and gave her the $50 bill on top of the soda cost. The woman even said something to her about being blessed. She tried to give the woman the $50 back when she realized when she got back inside to the cash register that the other "bill" was a 50, but the woman had already left.

Crazy, good stuff happens when you are obedient to the Word. We try to speak *life* always and when we catch each other speaking something negative into existence like "this day is going to be so hard," "I am getting sick," "I am so broke," etc., we stop each other and say, "Don't speak that out!" :-) And then we correct it with, "I'm going to have a great day," "I am so glad I am healed in Jesus's name and not sick," and "God is my provider, and I'm so thankful He gives me all I need."

Thought for the Day: God wants to bless us more than we want to receive. Speak things out that you desire! Speak positive! Get an accountability partner to help "catch" one another when something negative is spoken!

DAY 5

But I say to you, love your enemies, bless those who
curse you, do good to those who hate you, and pray for
those who spitefully use you and persecute you.

—Matthew 5:44

Yes, the Word really does say we are to *love* our enemies and pray for them! I truly thought this would be an impossible thing to do—love and pray for your *enemies*?! Those that hurt you, use you, say things about you, sabotage you, lie to you, cheat you, gossip about you? The answer is *yes*. Because you see, all of those hurtful human behaviors are *not* of God, and they are not the person themselves. They are from the enemy, Satan, the inner critic, the spirit of the *world*, and we must fight them *God's way* to win. So we *love* them, and we pray for their deliverance. It is God's desire for all creation to come find rest in Him.

I had a situation one time when someone was putting my son in danger. My son was a go-kart racer and raced around a track at speeds up to one hundred miles per hour. During one prefinal race, another driver was purposefully trying to mess up my son's driving and was "bumping" him with his kart on purpose and trying to run him off the road at top speeds. The race director and race referees did not seem to be doing anything about it! The prefinal ended, and my son came back to the pit very upset. My husband and his best friend (Pit Crew) were *very* angry and about to go give the other racer a piece of their mind. They were cussing. I was crying. *This was my child, and no one was going to harm my baby boy*, is what I was thinking. And *then*, the scripture about praying for your enemies came to my mind.

I stopped the two men from going over to the racer that was putting my son in danger—they were about to surely go off on him and cause a great ruckus. They were filled with anger and no telling what they were going to say or do! Through my tears, I said, "Guys, I think we need to pray about this situation. The Word says we are to *pray* for our enemies and love them." They seriously looked at me like I had gone wacko, but agreed to this approach. (Kudos to the Holy Spirit on *that* one!)

My husband, his best friend, my son, and I gathered around the kart and held hands—out in the open, where all could see (again, *kudos* to the Holy Spirit because that was so unlike my husband and his best friend). I prayed that God place a hedge of protection around my son. I lifted up the other boy and asked God to bless him and help him to understand that what he was doing was so dangerous. I said, "God, your Word says we are to pray for those that try to harm us, so that is what we are doing. Honor this prayer, Lord."

The final race began soon after. The other boy started bumping my son *again* and trying to run him off the track! I was like, *God, but we* prayed *for that boy to stop!* My heart was beating so fast, and I started to cry and was not understanding why my prayers were not being answered…and then, *just like that*, the race referee black-flagged that other young man and he was thrown out of the race and my son went on to *win*!

Praying and loving your enemies is not easy. It seemed illogical to allow my son to get out there again in harm's way, but I knew that God's Word is true, and He is not a man who should lie. Who knows what would have happened if we allowed our emotions to get the best of us and "cuss" the boy out, or if I had lost faith when the boy started to do the bumping again. Instead, we stopped, we prayed, and we listened to the Holy Spirit's promptings and obeyed, and it turned out God took care of something that we could not have if we responded with human emotion.

Thought for the Day: Is there someone you feel is "against" you and is always making you feel inadequate? Or is there a person who you feel might be putting you in harm's way? Or is there someone who just has different views than you do, political or religious, that you feel is your enemy? *Love* them, *pray* for them, and just watch what God will do!

DAY 6

And whatever you do, do it heartily, as to the Lord and not to men.

—Colossians 3:23

This scripture says *whatever* we do...*everything* we do, we are to do it full of heart as we are doing it for the *Lord* and not people. Wow, this one I know is a hard one for most people. It is our human instinct or tendency to want to get recognized by *people* for doing good, or to be rewarded with money or things. And we really do not think of our day-to-day actions as being done for the *Lord*. We are always looking for instant gratification that we feel only *man* is capable of giving, so when people do not recognize us or reward us, we then just tend to get upset and say things like, "He/She doesn't even recognize me for going above and beyond, so I'm just not going to do such and such anymore!" Or we think, *Since they won't do this for me, I'm not going to do that for them!*

I had a situation at work where God literally threw this scripture in my face! Ha! I had taken a promotion at work to manage a big new account. During the interview, I was told that I would get an increase in pay, but that pay increase would not start until the account was fully up and going and production was in full force.

I stayed late for weeks working with sales and our IT department and human resources to hire new people to get the account up and running smoothly. It was going great! I was building a great relationship with the new client, and the number of orders were increasing. I felt it was now time to ask for that raise that I was promised, so I approached my supervisor and asked her about it.

She came back a few hours later and said, "The person who interviewed you said that a pay increase was never discussed for this new position when he was talking to you about the job, so you will not be getting a pay increase." My heart dropped. I was *mad*—so mad in fact that I went to my office and packed up my belongings. I didn't speak to anyone about how upset I was before I left. I was determined that I was *not* going back to that place that had misled me and is now cheating me.

It was a Friday when I got that bad news. That night, I went to a church revival and was looking for some encouragement and guidance from the Lord. I was so distraught and hurt by what my workplace had done to me. It was a great night of worship and fellowship, but I was still feeling so low. The next morning, during my devotional time, I asked the Lord to help me in this situation. I needed some kind of guidance as to what I should do about work. I opened my Bible and there, right in front of my face was Colossians 3:23 telling me that everything I do I need to do it unto God and not man. I started bawling of course, and I knew that I had to go back to the office on Monday and continue to go above and beyond for this new client because my goal was to please God and not man.

About four weeks passed. A Christian friend popped her head in my office, and she said, "I heard in my spirit that today is your day." I was like, *Oh great! I receive that!* :-) It wasn't five minutes later that my supervisor called me and asked me to come to her office. I got there, and she proceeded to tell me that the person who interviewed me had a change of heart, and he had decided to give me a raise that was not only effective immediately, it was going to be retro and go back to the day I started the new position, so I was going to get all of that back pay. *Wow*, just *wow*. God is so good! Had I left at that day of disappointment and not turned to the Word for help and guidance on what to do, I would've missed that huge blessing!

Thought for the Day: When you do all things like you are doing them for the *Lord* and not for *man*, it is all being recorded by God, and you are storing treasures in Heaven. Try not to look for and expect recognition from *man*. *Know* and have *faith* that the Lord is the only *true* giver of blessings.

DAY 7

Give, and it will be given to you: good measure,
pressed down, shaken together, and running over will
be put into your bosom. For with the same measure
that you use, it will be measured back to you.

—Luke 6:38

I absolutely *love* to *give*. I am pretty sure that I got it from my daddy as he was always looking for someone he could help. I am glad that I "inherited" that spirit because a giving nature is critical to moving in God's kingdom and helping others to see how real God is.

I believe this scripture is referring to *that* kind of giving, the giving that is led by the Holy Spirit to increase God's kingdom. Helping others is always good, but God really wants people to depend on Him for their needs and in return see His glory. When we give when led by the Holy Spirit, there are incredible outcomes.

I was in a church service one time. It was in the summertime, and their AC unit was out. It was *hot* y'all. It was probably my third time to visit this church, and during the offering, I gave $100. As the offering basket was passed through the church, I heard in my spirit, *Give a $1,000.* I was like, *I don't think I'm hearing you correctly, God, I just saved that $1,000 to pay off my credit card.* Then I was moved to tears, got on my knees to pray, and heard very clearly again that I needed to *give* $1,000.

Through tears streaming down my face, I got my checkbook out and wrote the check for $1000. I then began to think seriously, *My husband is going to be so mad that I cannot pay off our credit card now.*

But, God, but, God, I am being obedient to the Holy Spirit, and Your Word says "give and it shall be given to you." You've got this God, right? :-)

A little while later, I was blown away by what the pastor stood up and said. He told the congregation that they had been praying for "extra" offering today so that they could get the A/C fixed, and the amount they needed "extra" was $1,100. *What?!* That was the *exact* amount that the Holy Spirit moved on me to give that day! I was moved to big tears again…but still just a little worried of what my husband was going to say about no longer having the $1,000 I had been saving to pay off our credit card. Well, I walk in the door from church that day, and I see a check sitting on the counter made out to my husband for $1,300. I said, "Honey, what is this check?" and he told me that someone randomly offered to purchase one of my son's old race motors that we never thought we could make money on! Ha! Hallelujah! Credit card can be paid off! Ha!

I told my husband the story about the offering and church, and he got tears in his eyes and said, "And look what God did. He gave it back to us plus a little *extra*."

Thought for the Day: Giving is *good*, but giving when led by the Holy Spirit helps others to see how *real* God is and that He hears their prayers. Practice "listening" to what the Holy Spirit is telling you to give. It does not have to be monetary. Sometimes they may just need a meal taken to them or a ride somewhere.

DAY 8

For I am persuaded that neither death nor life, nor angels nor principalities nor powers, nor things present nor things to come, nor height nor depth, nor any other created thing, shall be able to separate us from the love of God which is in Christ Jesus our Lord.

—Romans 8:38–39

So there is *nothing* according to the Word that can separate us from God's love. Wow, what about that sin I committed, Lord? What about that unforgiveness I'm holding on to? What about that crazy thing I did last night? What about, what about, what about…the list goes on. *He loves us. Period.* We are His children, and He knows we are in a human body that is constantly being tempted by the enemy and the flesh. Praise God for His *grace* for those whose hearts are turned toward Him.

I was eating at a Church's Chicken for lunch one day, and the young man at the counter was having a very difficult time. I mean, *very* difficult. He was messing up on every order. He was giving the wrong change back, the wrong beverages, you name it. He was messing up big-time.

During these mess-ups, the woman worker in the back was literally yelling at him and telling him how stupid he was and rolling her eyes and bad-mouthing him. He never once responded back to her with any type of retaliation. For the most part, the customers were actually taking it pretty well, too, because the young man kept profusely apologizing and worked hard to correct all of his mistakes.

As I ate my lunch and witnessed all of this, I heard the Holy Spirit whisper to me, "I want you to tell him that I love him, and I'm proud at the way he's handing things." I was like, *Here I go, I know that I have to do this in front of all of these people.* (At this juncture, I was getting better at being obedient to the Holy Spirit because it always seemed to work out good!) :-)

I walked up to the cash register beside the two ladies who were ordering, and I said, "Young man, you have been handling all of the mistakes you have been making with such kindness toward the customers, and you have not retaliated against the woman who is yelling at you in the back. The Lord wanted me to tell you that He *sees* this, and He *loves* you." His mouth fell *wide open*, and then he said, "Ma'am, but you don't know what I *did* last night." Without skipping a beat, I said, "Well, *God* does, and He wants you to know that it did not separate you from His love." The two ladies ordering shouted, "Amen!" Ha!

You see, the *devil* was tormenting this young man's mind with guilt and shame for whatever he might've done the night before, and it was causing him great angst and to make a great deal of mistakes. God wanted him to see that He knows everything about him and loves him despite of anything he might've done in his flesh. I prayed that a seed was planted, and the young man would be drawn to seek the Lord.

Thought for the Day: When you feel like you may have done something that caused the Lord to no longer love you, you *didn't*. There is nothing that can separate you from that *love*. Seek Him, learn what repentance means, and learn to capture those thoughts the enemy will put in your head and *cast them down*!

DAY 9

But do not forget to do good and to share, for
with such sacrifices God is well pleased.
—Hebrews 13:16

It is my desire to try and do as much good for others as I can. I was blessed with an inheritance after my daddy died in 2008, and I really prayed about how I could use some of that money to bless others. In comes a lady from my workplace. She was raising her grandchildren and appeared so happy doing so, but it was no secret that she was strapped for cash and needed financial assistance.

My first experience helping her was with church camp for her grandchildren. I provided the "cash" that they would need to purchase food and snacks in the camp store. A second time I was led to help her was with purchasing groceries. She gave me directions to her home, and I delivered the groceries. Her grandchildren were so grateful and kind when I arrived, especially since I included a few junk food items. :-)

A couple of months after delivering the groceries, I was driving down the street, and I received this overwhelming urge to give this woman and her grandchildren a certain amount of money. It was so overwhelming that tears came to my eyes as I called my husband to tell him and get his blessing to provide this money.

It was a Sunday afternoon, so there were not any banks open. My husband reminded me of the cash we had set aside in the safe inside our home. I went home, gathered the money in an envelope, and drove to her house. I was not able to let her know that I was coming because she could no longer afford a phone. Thankfully, I remembered where she lived since I had delivered the groceries there a couple of months prior.

I arrived to her house, and she answered the door and was surprised to see me. I let her know that God had led me there with an urgent need to provide her with an envelope with a certain amount of money. We both were crying and overwhelmed at how cool God is—it ended up being the *exact* amount that she needed to pay some medical bills for her grandson that *had* to be paid the following day. *Praise the Lord!* She had been praying to God for a miracle, and He delivered.

Thought for the Day: God will use us to answer people's prayers and to show them how *real* He is. We must *stop, pray, listen,* and *obey.* Do good and *share* when prompted by the Holy Spirit.

DAY 10

Again I say to you that if two of you agree on
earth concerning anything that they ask, it will be
done for them by My Father in heaven.

—Matthew 18:19

It took me a little while to fully understand this scripture and a few other scriptures that state that "God will answer your prayers *if* you agree, *if* you seek Me, *if* you ask in Jesus's name, *if* you have the faith of a mustard seed, etc." I found the "key" was the word *if*. When we pray, we have to make sure our motivation behind it is always *God's will* and not just our own "wishes." We need to be in agreement with Jesus. We need to seek God in His scriptures and in relationship to understand how to pray.

I have a great testimony of Christians coming together to pray in this manner, and then those prayers being answered by my Father in heaven. It was concerning our home that was in great need of repairs because it had been purchased as a foreclosure. We needed a new roof but could not afford one. One afternoon, my husband walked out to the front fence and found a flyer from a roofing company called Integrity. He said, "Honey, I feel like I need to call these guys to come look at our roof."

Integrity Roofing came out to our home in the next few days, took a look at our roof, and told my husband it was in really bad shape and definitely needed replacement. It was all preexisting damage, so it was highly unlikely that insurance would cover it.

The gentlemen from Integrity walked into our home with my husband to discuss a little further. The owner of the roofing company saw the wall in our living room that was covered in crosses and a scripture. He asked my husband, "Are you believers?" And my husband said, "Oh yes, definitely." He asked my husband if they could pray together in agreement about the roof, and they joined hands and prayed for the Lord's favor in our roof situation. I got home from work and was so happy to hear this had happened!

The insurance company showed up in the next few days to walk the roof and assess the damage. I was home this time, and Integrity Roofing was present as well. It was crazy, but our conversation naturally leaned toward Jesus, and we were in agreement about how He can do the impossible for His people. We exchanged stories about what the Lord had done for our families.

When the assessment was complete, the insurance company made the decision that our roof was a total loss—even calling it a catastrophe—and that it needed to be replaced. They were going to cover it *all*. *Hallelujah!* They also determined our barn roof was a catastrophe as well and were going to cover it to be totally replaced as well.

What a blessing this was! And we learned that the owner of Integrity was actually a minister for the Lord. He discipled young men who had been in trouble and rejected, and he gave them an opportunity to work and build their faith life. Everyone involved was in agreement with the Lord's ways. It is incredible what God can do with the power of agreement in prayer!

Thought for the Day: Look for Jesus in everything you do. He *is* all and wants to be involved in *everything* we do! Share your faith—it is amazing what believers can accomplish *together* in agreement as long as they are in agreement with God's will.

DAY 11

Confess your faults one to another, and pray one for
another, that ye may be healed. The effectual fervent
prayer of a righteous man availeth much.

—James 5:16

Here's another scripture about praying for one another. It's so important to pray, especially when led by the Holy Spirit to do so. The Holy Spirit is that internal voice from God that His Word says He equips us with once we believe in Jesus in our heart. Occasionally, the Holy Spirit will give us visions and dreams that we most definitely need to pay attention to.

One night, I was awakened by what I thought was an audible voice that said the name *Jane*. I turned to my husband to see if he had said anything, but he was fast asleep. I then "saw" this name written, and I knew immediately who it was for because it was spelled out J-A-Y-N-E in cursive letter "lights," so to speak. I asked the Lord, "What am I to pray for Jayne?" and I heard in my spirit the words *ankle replacement*. I was like, *What?!* I've heard of knee and hip replacements, but never an "ankle"!

I began to pray for God to touch Jayne by His healing power and replace her ankle! I felt a little crazy, but I was thinking, *I didn't just see and hear that for nothing!* Who has thoughts of *ankle* replacement healings?! I thanked God for using my vessel to pray for her, and then I went back to sleep.

Jayne was someone I worked with, so the next morning, as I got ready for work, I was praying to God and asking if I was supposed to let Jayne know what happened. I had learned that sometimes God shows me people to pray for, but does not lead me to tell them about it. Well, this time, I felt in my spirit that He wanted me to *tell* her. I asked God to make it easy for me (ha!) and let her receive and not think I'm a wacko! :-)

I got to work and went by her desk and told her to stop by and see me when she had a chance because I had something to share with her. She followed me to my desk right then. We got into my office, and I told her what had happened in the middle of the night—I didn't hold back. She began to cry and let me know that *no one* knew this, but she had been praying to God about her ankle because it had been bothering her so much. With tears in my eyes, I said, "Let's pray now!"

The Holy Spirit fell, and I laid my hands on her ankle and thanked God for the *ankle replacement*. She has not had any pain since, and there are times I would walk by her desk and we would just look at each other and get so tickled at what God did. She said that this experience increased her *faith* for sure because she was questioning if God even *knew* her or was pleased with her, and *now* she knows *he knows her by name* and loves her so much. He used a willing vessel to *pray* for her.

Thought for the Day: If you ever get the whim to pray for someone, like their name or face pops in your head, then *do it*. You just never know the impact God's power through *you* may have. People need these kinds of experiences to know how *real* He is.

DAY 12

This is My commandment, that you love
one another as I have loved you.

—John 15:12

*L*ove one another. This means everyone. Even the unlovable? *Yes.* After all, as we read there in John, it is a *commandment.* It is not always easy to show love, especially in public when people are acting all crazy, and it seems trying to provoke us into saying or doing something that we cannot take back and serves no purpose.

I was at our local theme park with a young lady one afternoon, and I was really tested in this area. We were waiting in a really long line at a roller coaster, and there was a group of young teenage boys and girls in line behind us. I would guess that they were around twelve to thirteen years old. One of the young boys was using profanity and talking so vulgar. It was offensive language toward one of the young ladies with them, and I almost turned around and said, "Young man, I really do not appreciate you talking like that." And then I heard the Holy Spirit.

"Tammy, I need you to lay your hands on that young man and tell him that I love him." Say what?! *Surely* I was *not* hearing the spirit of the Lord *this* time. As we moved up the line, the Holy Spirit continued to nudge me, and I was like, *God, I need a* sign *if I am to say anything.* Now, I know I shouldn't be "bargaining" with God and needed to just be *obedient*, when all of a sudden, I heard one of the other young men with the group say to the vulgar talking one, "Man, you need to stop talking like that. There are people all around us."

I took that *very perfect* moment to turn around, and I said, "Young man, I am a minister, and the Lord wants you to know that *He loves you*." His eyes got so big, and I asked if I could lay my hands on him and ask God to bless him. The other young man, also with eyes wide open, said, "Well, God doesn't love me…" It was a perfect opportunity to tell them *both* that He sure does and that there was nothing that they could do or say to stop His love.

I laid my hands on them and asked God to bless them. *Total silence* now as we made our way up the steep ramp to get on the ride. The top of the ride was about two or three stories high. When we got to the top and the line stopped for a little while, the vulgar-talking young man proceeds to sit atop the railing and what took place next still blows me away to this day. You see, the young man started to fall backward down two stories to the ground when supernaturally he was picked up and placed on his feet. The group was *stunned*, including my young friend and me! *God saved this boy from falling, and he knew it.* The young people just started talking about God and what had just happened, and I could tell that this incident was going to stick with them forever as well too. They saw how real God was.

Now, had I gone all religious on this young man and took offence and told him to "stop talking that way," he would have never experienced this type of *love* of God. I prayed (and still pray) for this young man to always remember the incident and realize God's love for him is real, and God has a work for him to do.

Thought for the Day: Listen for the Holy Spirit's promptings. There are people *everywhere* that we can impact with God's *love*. People need to see God for who He really is and not see Him as some entity out there who wants you to follow all these rules, or talk a certain way, or do a certain thing before He will ever love you.

DAY 13

And we know that all things work together for good to those who love God, to those who are the called according to *His* purpose.

—Romans 8:28

This scripture just makes us cringe at times because we know there are going to be bad things that happen to us, and it's very hard sometimes to believe that God can really work all that *bad* for our *good*. Now, I believe there are some "bad" things we won't see worked out for our good until we are with Him in heaven and see the "aha" moments of why things had to happen the way they did while on earth, but praise God we are able to see some of the good *now*.

I was able to witness a "sick child" situation being turned into something good, but it did not come without suffering and doubt and worry, *believe* me! After all, this was my *child* and seeing him in pain was *not* what I would've chosen. He became very ill one May, and we suspected meningitis. Sure enough, after the hospital tests, we discovered it was indeed meningitis.

After a couple of days of suffering, I felt the Holy Spirit urge me to lay my hands on him for healing. Immediately after I did this, he threw up and became a different child. He felt great, had friends over, and seemed totally healed. I believe that God healed him through the laying on of hands. We were so happy and relieved!

The very next morning, I went back to his room to check on him, and he was just waking up. I crawled into the bed, and we started watching a video on his computer. A little while later, he stood up out of bed and *dropped to his knees* in pain and cried out,

"Mom! We need to go to the hospital! My head, my head, my head!" I was like, *What is happening? My son is* healed. I called his doctor, and he said to get to the hospital immediately. My son became so "out of it," and I thought the trip to the hospital was the longest trip of my life!

They got him back right away and starting IVs and testing. They said he was extremely dehydrated, and tests showed that he had a "mass" at the base of his brain, and they wanted to transport him by ambulance to Dallas Children's Medical Center ASAP. We got to the hospital room and waited for the MRI they said was needed. The night went by…the next day went by…another day went by…still no MRI, and the only way my son was comfortable was lying down. Every time he'd get up, he was in excruciating pain. The MRI was "delayed" due to all of the other children's cases that were coming in that were "more critical."

I kept praying and trusting God that he had *already healed* my son. My son and I were witnessing to the nurses in the hospital, and they were amazed at my son's attitude. *But* it was starting to get a bit ridiculous that we had been in the hospital now for four days with no MRI. I thanked God that my son's case was not considered critical like those other children that were coming in, but I did ask to see patient relations to discuss the delay. They came and were very apologetic and said that they would get my son in by midnight that night.

The MRI showed that when my son had gone through the spinal fluid test for meningitis the week prior, they had poked so many holes in his spinal sack that the fluid had all leaked out and was "pooling" at the base of his neck (the "mass" they saw at the first hospital). They said what had been happening is that every time he stood up, his brain had no fluid cushion, so it was causing the excruciating pain! (Wow!) There was no more meningitis, of course. I knew he was *healed* from that! :-)

The treatment for my son's issue was for them to pump caffeine into his body, and he had to lie completely *flat* for forty-eight hours for the holes in the spinal sack to heal. *My son did it!* (I know it had to be with God's help.)

The story doesn't stop there—I still have to get to where "God worked it all out for our good." You see, we had a big family cruise planned that was supposed to start the day my son got out of the hospital. We ended up having to cancel it earlier in the week because we were not sure what was going to happen with my son. My mom lost all of the money she paid for the cruise line because she had not taken the insurance. There were many sad people—ten in all were supposed to go on that trip.

Well, we got home from the hospital (when we were supposed to be on the ship), and our lights in the house start to "flicker." My husband said, "This can't be good," and he checked the internal electrical box, and all seemed fine. The lights flickered again, and my husband went outside to check the external electrical box, and it was smoking! He was able to catch it in enough time before bursting into flames. *Had we not been home*, our house would've burnt to the ground.

So you see, my son's illness, the delay at the hospital, cancelling the cruise—all those things worked for our *good* because we didn't lose our home. *And* my mom ended up making all of the cruise money back in stock trading! *To God be the glory!*

Thought for the Day: No matter how bad things may look, keep praying, keep trusting God, keep referring to scripture, and know that if you love God and are called according to His purpose, He *will* work it *all* out for your good.

DAY 14

Be anxious for nothing, but in everything by prayer and supplication, with thanksgiving, let your requests be made known to God; and the peace of God, which surpasses all understanding, will guard your hearts and minds through Christ Jesus.
—Philippians 4:6–8

I think I came out of the womb worrying and full of fear. My mom said I started worrying about pleasing others and what they thought of me from a very early age. This is really not healthy thinking and can really mess with your physical health as well. I ended up getting an ulcer when I was only eleven years old!

So I grew up constantly being concerned if I was going to be liked, or was doing everything right, and it made me start reading too much into what people said. I seemed to always take all complaints personally and went way over and above at times trying to figure out what I might've done wrong and how I could make it better.

Praise God that after I started a relationship with Him, He began to show me that being anxious, or worrying, *does no good.* And He showed me that there is an anointing in the word *no!* I had to stop being so concerned that if I did not do or say or act like *they* thought I should, they may not like me. I learned I am living to please my Father in Heaven, *not* man, and *man's* ways are not always pleasing to God. I "trained" myself that as soon as the anxiety started, I would *stop* and pray with thanksgiving and let *God* show me if I did anything wrong. He brought such a *peace* in those situations when I followed this scripture.

The workplace is somewhere that I have really put this scripture to good use. I work in a place dominated by men, and those I work closest with have titles like director and executive or senior vice president. I want to please them, truly I do, but I must discern if what they are asking me to do or say is what *God* would want me to do or say!

A perfect example is when I worked very closely with one of the gentlemen on one of our largest client accounts. The monthly calibration meetings with the client were typically uncomfortable, and he dominated the conference calls. At times, he made it seem as though *we* were the client, and he was displeased with the requests that the client was asking us to do! I began to worry, started taking it on myself thinking this client is going to be mad at *me* for his behavior, and then I *stopped*, I *prayed*, and just thanked God for being able to work on this account and asked Him to reveal what was happening in this uncomfortable relationship with one of our largest clients.

Wow. God brought such a *peace* after I prayed, and then He did something for me I never thought could happen (and it would not have happened had I continued handling it with anxiety and worry). You see, the client reached out to their account manager a week or so after I prayed about it and asked for the gentlemen who had been dominating those client meetings to be removed from their account! They requested that I run those monthly conference calls from then on!

Thought for the Day: Worry and anxiety *does no good*. Pleasing others by agreeing to do or say what *they* do and say *does no good*. We must *pray* as soon as we start to feel anxious or when we discern that something is not right. We must give God *thanks* and let our requests be made known to *him*, and He is guaranteed to guard our hearts and work it out for us.

DAY 15

I can do all things through Christ who strengthens me.
—Philippians 4:13

This scripture is a lot of people's favorite, including mine. When Paul was talking to the Philippians, he was explaining to them that now, after truly seeing who Christ was and the power that came from knowing *Him*, he could be content in *all* circumstances because when Christ is "with" us, He truly does give us a supernatural ability to "get through things"—good or bad.

I've been through good and bad times when I've leaned on this scripture. Several of the "bad" times have been through deaths of friends and family members. Speaking at those memorial services was not something I thought I could get through. God truly did give me His strength, and I was able to read scriptures that I was lead to by God, and I was able to speak of wonderful memories of those loved ones.

I've also leaned on this scripture for good scenarios, like being asked to *pray in public—yikes*. I really didn't think I would *ever* be able to do *that* and certainly not be comfortable doing it. He reminded me, "You can do all things through *Me*, I will give you strength." The first couple of times were terrifying, ha! I was not fully letting Him give me *strength*. I was too much in my flesh wondering "what everyone was going to think." I felt like I was going to sound stupid and certainly felt like I was not going to be "biblically" correct in my prayers!

With *His* strength though, I've realized that praying is not perfect. It's not rehearsed, it is *just talking to God*. I can do it because it's through *Him* and His strength that I am doing it, and it is *pleasing* to Him, no matter what it sounds like.

Thought for the Day: Recite this scripture whenever you feel like *you* are not able to do something—because you know what? "You" (your flesh) could very well be getting in the way of doing something you need to do. Remember, *He* gives us strength, and *He* can get us through *all* things as long as our focus is on Him.

DAY 16

Rejoice always, pray continually, give thanks in all
circumstances;for this is God's will for you in Christ Jesus.
—1 Thessalonians 5:16–18

This is going to be short today, but one of the most important things to understand. God wants us to *pray continually* and be happy and thankful always. *It's His will* for us. This particular scripture was written on the church wall where I used to attend when I was into "religion" (not relationship). When I'd pass by it, I would just think to myself, *There is no way I can get on my knees and pray continually... really God?!*

As I began to get into a relationship with God (and not religion), I realized one does not have to be on their knees or have their eyes closed to pray! I decided I needed some sort of "reminder" that would help me to pray continually. Of course, not in a mindless tradition sort of way that ends up being routine, but just something that would "get me going" and get me into the mind-set of continually talking to God.

So this is what I did.

Each morning as I got dressed, I would let parts of my daily routine "remind" me what to pray about:

As I opened my eyes, I would say thank you for a good night's rest.

As I washed my skin, I would say, God, clean my insides (my heart) too.

As I put on my mascara, I would thank God for opening my eyes to understanding.

As I brushed my teeth, I would ask Him to let wholesome talk come out of my mouth.

As I brushed my hair, I would say thank you for knowing every hair on my head.

As I got dressed, I would say thank you for clothing me with your righteousness.

As I put on my shoes, I would say, order my steps, Lord.

It became a way of life—it prompted me to begin to continue this prayer life *all day long*. And God started answering those prayers and talking back to me! It wasn't like the movie *The Ten Commandments* when Moses would hear God's audible voice. God answered through people, songs, scripture, in my inner thoughts. Signs, miracles, and wonders began to follow me, and it was all because of *continual communing/prayer with God*.

Thought for the Day: Pray. Pray. Pray. And then pray some more. :-)

DAY 17

For you can all prophesy one by one, that all
may learn and all may be encouraged.
—1 Corinthians 14:31

Now this is a scripture that I was never taught or never even heard about when I was into religion. I thought this type of thing (prophesy) only happened in the Old Testament like with men named Isaiah, Ezekiel, Jeremiah, etc. Or I thought people who claimed to prophesy this day and time must also be speaking in tongues (we'll talk about that another day) or dancing with snakes. Ha!

Not so. One of the most incredible days of my life was when a woman of God was obedient and gave me a "word from God." It knocked my socks off. This woman read my mail y'all! She came up to me and basically described a whole scenario in my life that had happened a couple of days before that caused me great angst. I thought there was no way God even had a clue what I was going through, and the pain that was in my heart. This woman of God showed me *God was real* and truly must know every hair on my head.

It was amazing, eye-opening, the coolest thing that ever happened to me...that God would use another vessel to let me know *He saw everything* that happened to me that night, and He's going to make it better. *Hope*...I now had *hope*.

I would encourage you to read more about prophecy in the Bible. It is real, and God intends for His people to prophesy to build each other up. It is not "hokey," and it has *nothing* to do with being psychic or being any kind of medium. Those people are *not of God*, and their purpose in "reading your mail" does *nothing* to glorify God. Prophecy is a God-given gift, and its sole purpose is to encourage and build up the body of Christ.

There are "false prophets" out there who say that they are doing it in the name of Jesus, but their motives are wrong. A prophet of God will never give a Word to God's people in hopes of getting money in return. The motivation of a prophet of God will always be to build *the* Kingdom of God and *encourage* others.

Thought for the Day: Don't discount prophecy. It is *real,* and God uses this gifting to encourage and build up His people.

DAY 18

My brethren, count it all joy when you fall into various trials,
knowing that the testing of your faith produces patience.
—James 1:2–3

Really, God, you want us to count *trials* as joy? That's a tough one
to swallow, but I have learned to do it. A trial I'm remembering now
was one of the first ones where I learned to *speak life* and continue to
be joyful and *not* look at my circumstance.

The doctor called after my annual "lady" exam and said that I
needed to go in for a second mammogram. They found some suspi-
cious spots, five spots in fact. I couldn't get in for the second mammogram and hospital testing for about a week. The worry, of course,
started to set in immediately. *What are my kids going to do without me
if I die?!* Then I *stopped*, I *prayed*, I *listened*, and I heard, *Count it all
joy when you fall in various trials.*

I *obeyed* that scripture. I began to *thank God* for my complete
healing. I began to *speak life* that I was going to *live* and surely not
die. I continually thanked the Lord that He has *already* healed me.
I asked God to increase my faith and let this trial show how faithful
He is.

I arrived at the hospital, and the mammogram technician took
me back to the room with the lovely "smasher" machine. When I
walked in to that room, there, just glaring at me, was the computer
monitor. Five big red circles around my "spots" from my first breast
X-ray. I said, "Is that my x-ray from before?" and the lady said yes
then pushed me along to the "smasher" to get more pictures. I have to

say, the panic started to "set in" again after seeing those big red circles on that screen…but I captured those thoughts again and thanked God again for my healing.

The technician ended up having to move my breasts in all sorts of "angles" to keep getting more and more and more pictures. The doctor kept calling up there and asking her to get "one more"—it felt like at least fifteen more times. She then told me that the doctor said that she needs to look at my breasts with a sonogram, so we moved to another room. My mom got to come in that room with me.

The doctor ended up having to take about a half a dozen sonograms of my breasts. I kept saying, "May I get dressed now?" and the technician would tell me, "Not yet." I looked at my mom between the last two sonograms and said, "There must be so many more spots now since she's having to look so many times…" I then started to talk about death, and I told my mom that I wasn't scared to die, I just was sad for my babies if I were to leave them. My *mom* this time said, "*Stop* that talk!" And again, this scripture came to mind to count the trial as *joy*, but it was *hard* y'all!

I could finally get dressed, and I waited what seemed like hours for the doctor to come talk to me. She finally arrived and with a "sour" look on her face (I kid you not), and she said, "I couldn't find anything." The technician literally jumped up and down, hugged my neck, and said, "Praise the Lord!" (We both had professed our love for the Lord earlier during the whole "picture" process.)

You see, the doctor had to look *so many times* at my breasts because *there was nothing there anymore, y'all.* It was so strange that she seemed so "irritated" about it, but I am thinking it's because of the "proof" that the spots were *there* before, and with them now unable to be found, it might be seen as she failed in some way. I prayed that a seed was planted as the technician, my mom, and I rejoiced in the Lord.

Thought for the Day: Trials are going to come, it's inevitable. If God can get even one seed planted in a nonbeliever from the results of your reaction to that trial, it's really all worth it. Every time I'm in a trial, I turn to God and say, "Can't wait to see what You're going to do with *this* one, help me to be full of faith, Lord, and *count it all joy.*"

DAY 19

But Jesus looked at them and said to them, "With men this
is impossible, but with God all things are possible."
—Matthew 19:26

Love this scripture now that I understand it! I used to get so disappointment when I didn't achieve something that I wanted to achieve, and it made me question if God *was* really "with" me since I didn't accomplish exactly what I wanted to accomplish! This scripture is not just a phrase that gives you a guarantee that you can accomplish whatever it is *you* want to accomplish in your *flesh*, it pertains to all things in God's Will are possible!

The testimony that comes to my mind with this scripture is about my brother. My brother was estranged from our family for more than twenty years. He was deep in addiction, and it had gotten him into a lot of trouble, even jail time. It cost him his relationships with family, his job, and his home. I believe the most heartbreaking for him is that our father passed away before he was able to get free from the addiction and could fully restore the awesome relationship that he had with him. This made my brother very sad.

Thankfully, the Lord pursued my brother relentlessly, and he was moved by the Holy Spirit to get help from a Bible-based rehabilitation home. He began to reach out to me and my mom again and restore all relationships with his family. He had nothing to call his own, but he knew he had *God*, and as his faith increased, he continued to seek the Lord. He began to see the Lord move in his life and show him favor.

The first Christmas rolled around during his restoration period, and my brother was staying at my house for a couple of weeks. We were up late talking about God one night and how good He had been to my brother, and he just kept repeating, "With God, all things are possible." You see, my brother was beginning to now live a life of *God's Will* and *not* his own fleshly will.

Just before bedtime, my brother asked for a Bible to read—I had just the one! My son had inherited our father's Bible, and now that my son knew his uncle was recovered, he had wrapped it up and put it under the tree for him!

I looked at my brother with giddiness, and I asked him if he wanted an early Christmas present, and I proceeded to get the Bible out from under the tree. He unwrapped it, and we both cried. He began to thumb through the Bible to see if our dad had anything notated or written in it and lo and behold, there it was.

The only thing my dad had written or highlighted in that entire Bible was, you guessed it, Matthew 19:26! *With God all things are possible.* It was the coolest, best moment *ever* shared with my brother, *knowing* that surely God was with us and wanted us to know the forgiveness of a *father*.

Thought for the Day: The written Word of God restores, it brings life, it brings love. God has so much for us to accomplish in His will, and all of it is possible if you seek Him!

DAY 20

If we live in the Spirit, let us also walk in the Spirit.

—Galatians 5:25

"Walking in the spirit" was such a foreign thing to me when I was living in the "good deeds" of religion just trying to do good, do good, do good. I learned that the deeds that may look "good" are not necessarily *God*. He wants to get us in such a place where we are being led by Him and doing what *He* wants us to do so that we are able to show others how real He is!

Walking in the spirit means listening for all the promptings from the inner guide that God has instilled in each believer, the Holy Spirit. Now, the Holy Spirit is not going to guide you to do anything that does not line up with the Word of God. Walking in the spirit will always produce fruit of the spirit…love, joy, patience, kindness, etc.

Listening for this inner guidance can change your well thought-out plans, even for lunch, ha! One day, I was in the drive-through line for a popular sandwich place (it was "lent" season, and I wanted shrimp, and it was the only time this sandwich shop had shrimp), when I heard the promptings of the Holy Spirit to go to a different dine-in restaurant down the street. I really wanted that shrimp, and I was in between cars, so I just stayed in the line.

Lo and behold, I get up to the drive-through speaker, only to find out that they were *out of shrimp*. Okay, Holy Spirit, forgive me. I hear you loud and clear now, and I will go to the dine-in restaurant! :-)

I arrived to what I would call kind of a chaotic atmosphere—just a heaviness and not much joy seen in the staff or the customers. They sat me at a booth, and I was greeted by a young lady *full of light*. (I think that she was the only one in there that smiled at me.) She was all tattooed up, nose ring, blue hair, and some heavy eyeliner, but she had *joy*, *kindness*, and just a sparkle of light!

She took my order, and as I waited for my food, I heard in my spirit that this young lady was going through some of the worst times of her life and wasn't quite sure how she was going to survive. In my spirit, I was like, *But, God, she is so full of light and love and joy!* I was being prompted to let her know that He sees her overcoming spirit and is so proud of her for not allowing all of her problems to affect her service.

She brought me my food, and I began to eat. The Holy Spirit kept prompting me, *Tell her, tell her, tell her.* When she came back around the next time, I told her that I was so impressed with her wonderful customer service and how joyful she was. I told her that the Lord laid on my heart to tell her that He sees this and knows that although she is in some of the worst times of her life, He is so proud that she is able to overcome and treat others with kindness.

Her mouth literally dropped open. She slid in the booth with me and said, "Who are you?! How do you know that?!" I said, "I love the Lord, and He uses me sometimes to show people how real He is and to show them that He sees them and is proud when they overcome. He sees that you love Him and are trying to do the next right thing." We hugged, we cried, and I truly believe she got a glimpse of the real God, and a seed was planted.

I went back to the restaurant a few months later and asked for her. The waitress I asked said, "Are you the church lady that spoke to her here about Jesus one day?" I told her it was indeed me! :-) She said that the young lady had told her about it, and it affected her in a great way and that she was doing very well. It blessed me tremendously.

Thought for the Day: The Holy Spirit's plan is always better than our own. He wants to guide us into all truth and help others understand the love of God and how real He is. (And the plan just might end up getting you what *you* desire. You see, the dine-in restaurant had *shrimp*.) :-)

DAY 21

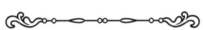

If we live in the Spirit, let us also walk in the Spirit.
—Galatians 5:25

I am staying on this theme to share another beautiful time that the Holy Spirit prompted me to speak to a server at a restaurant. This happens to be one of my most favorite way God uses me. Out there in the real world. To talk to people who might not ever step foot in a church.

I was at lunch with a good friend at a favorite local restaurant. They took us to a table in a back room with a huge table full of the Red Hat ladies. (If you don't know who they are, I would encourage you to google it—ha!) These ladies were being unbelievably demanding of this young man: lunch too cold, not enough mustard, need more tea, you forgot my French fries, etc. The young man looked over at us and politely said, "I'm sorry for the wait, I will be right with you."

He continued to serve the demanding Red Hats with such kindness and grace. I heard the spirit of the Lord whisper, "He is gay, and I love him so much." I thought, *Wow, okay, Lord, where are we going with this one?* He then came over to take our order (finally—ha!), and I heard the spirit of the Lord say to me, "I want you to tell him how much I love him." Wow…uh, okay, Lord, give me a minute to process this.

By the time he delivered our food, the Red Hats had left the backroom, and it was just the waiter, me, and my friend in that backroom of the restaurant. I looked him in the eye, and I said, "You are a precious young man, and the Lord wanted me to tell you that He loves you." Tears welled up in his eyes, and we hugged in silence for what felt like a full hour. I could *feel* the hurt streaming from his body.

He proceeded to tell me that he was gay and that he grew up in a church family that no longer receives him because of his lifestyle. He said when he was much younger, they got him in a circle in the middle of the church and tried to cast the "gay demons" out of him. It shook him and his faith to the core, and he certainly now thought that God could no longer love someone who had these "demons."

I gently explained to him that mankind and the world is full of all sorts of demons—pride, lust, anger, envy, addiction, gluttony, religiosity, etc., but that does not separate us from the *love* of God. I encouraged him to seek God and pray and then the Holy Spirit will shine the light on all truth what he needed to know.

Thought for the Day: We must be led by the Holy Spirit, especially with something like "casting out demons." We can cause more harm to people than good. *There is nothing that separates man from the love God.*

DAY 22

Start children off on the way they should go, and even
when they are old they will not turn from it.
—Proverbs 22:6

W hen my children were born, it was instant love for me. When
I would look at them, I would ask God to help me be the kind of
mother He wanted me to be. The love I felt brought almost a "lump"
to my throat. I would sing Jesus songs to them as I nursed them, and
I would just cry in awe that I was so blessed to be their mother.

I was constantly stroking their sweet little face and head and
holding and loving on them. Even as they got older, when they were
around me, I was constantly touching them to stroke their hair or
scratch their back or hug on them. I even had a couple of people
point out to me, "You are always touching your children," like it was
"weird" or something. Little did I know that it was just unusual to
most people to do this.

I tried to only give words of encouragement to my children
rather than any words that would discourage them or tear them
down. I always looked them in the eye and gave them my undivided
attention. I felt my children were gifts from God.

One day when my kids were in their teens, I was just praising
God in tears for how proud I was of them. They both had always
made such good choices, were so responsible, respectful of all those
in authority, got themselves up for school, made awesome grades,
and were genuinely *kind*. Through my tears, I asked God, "How did

I get so blessed that they turned out like this?" and the Lord showed me a vision.

The vision was me washing dishes at the sink when my daughter was about three years old. She was tugging at my pants leg. I turned off the water, dried off my hands and bent down on her level, looked her in the eyes and said, "What do you need, baby?" I then heard the spirit of the Lord say, "*That* is why, you gave them *you* and your undivided attention."

Our children need *us*. They need to feel loved at all times. They don't have to be your own. They *want* to do good when they have this confidence of being loved like the Father in heaven loves *us*. That is what I've learned—to train a child up in *love*, and they *will never depart from it*.

Thought for the Day: Love, love, love. *That* is God's way, and children will never want to depart from it.

DAY 23

Let us not become weary in doing good, for at the proper time we will reap a harvest if we do not give up.
—Galatians 6:9

I love this scripture! Many times it is so hard to keep doing good, especially toward a specific person, when you seem to not get anything in return. This is how I felt for quite a few years toward my husband. I felt like I was always doing things the way he wanted me to do them, but yet he never returned the good. I felt it was pretty much "his way or the highway"! :-)

I found myself becoming so bitter as I folded his clothes the way he wanted them, as I loaded the dishwasher the way he wanted it, as I laid the coffee spoon the way he wanted it, etc. Through gritted teeth, sometimes I was doing these things for him, and my thoughts always went to, *He does nothing in return for me!* I would truly fall into a self-pity, and it was making me physically sick, I feel like!

One day, as I folded his socks perfectly with feelings of anger behind it, I heard the spirit of the Lord say, "Do you love him?" And I was like, *Of course, I love my husband, Lord!* And I heard Him say, "Then what difference does it make if you do these things for him. If you *love* someone, you do those things *because* of that love." Wow.

I started my journey of doing these good things for my husband with joy in my heart and *because I loved him*. No other reason. The "weariness" went away, and I was now doing these things with sincere joy in my heart. The harvest was that inner *joy* that I now had, and it brought such *peace* to our household.

I learned to start *letting go* of the things that used to irritate me about my husband, like leaving his clothes all over the bedroom floor, leaving on lights, or dipping snuff. I would hear the Lord say again as I started to get irritated, "Do you love him?" Yes, I do, Lord. "Then what difference does it make?" No one is perfect, and there are going to be things about each other that husbands and wives just don't like!

Thought for the Day: A harvest of *joy* and *peace* can be reaped if we learn to not grow weary in doing good. Do those good things from a place of *love*!

DAY 24

Whoever oppresses the poor shows contempt for their Maker, but whoever is kind to the needy honors God.
—Proverbs 14:31

There are people in need all around us. Some are obvious, some not so much, and so the prompting of the Holy Spirit can be so very powerful to those in need and can show them how *real* God is.

I was in line at the grocery store loading my groceries on the conveyor belt. I looked at the cashier and smiled, and I heard the Holy Spirit's prompting that the young lady was in desperate need for money. I began my conversation with God and was asking Him if I was to give her some money. I was thinking to myself, *Really, God, the cashiers are not supposed to take tips probably.*

I then heard in my spirit, "Give her everything in your wallet." Here comes my thoughts: *But I just went to the bank, God. That money is for the kids and I to go to the movies and buy goodies later.* Again, I heard, "Give her everything in your wallet." *But, God, how do I just reach over and give her this money?*

There we were at the end of the transaction, and I'm just staring at the cashier. I reached into my wallet, grabbed her hand, and put the cash in it and told her, "The Lord asked me to bless you with the cash that was in my wallet." She looked at me in disbelief and began to cry.

She proceeded to tell me that while she was ringing up my groceries, she was so concerned thinking about how she was going to get home to her baby after work. She had no money, no gas, and no food. But *God* knew, *God* heard her, and *God* provided.

I began to see this young lady at the grocery store often. She would often ask me to pray for this or that. She told me that she was attending church, and she seemed so full of joy every time I'd see her!

She ended up giving back to *me* as well. Not financially, but with the Holy Spirit's prompting, she encouraged me to do a "wellness check" the grocery store was having. They took my blood pressure. It turned out that it was very high! I had no idea! This prompted me to get it checked out. I am so grateful that God had our paths cross!

Thought for the Day: It is so important to help the needy, especially when prompted by the Holy Spirit. When we help others, we are helping ourselves as well and are honoring God!

DAY 25

> If anyone has material possessions and sees a
> brother or sister in need but has no pity on them,
> how can the love of God be in that person?
> —1 John 3:17

I am the first one to always want to *give*, especially to those in need. I have learned though to really listen to the Holy Spirit's prompting when it comes to giving because God always has a plan to make Himself known, and I really do not want to "mess that up" by giving "too soon" or "too much."

Let me tell you a story that will explain what I mean. I worked with a godly woman, and she and her husband's only car had broken down. She lived somewhat close to me, and she asked me if I could take her to and from work until the car got fixed, and I said yes.

After about a week of driving her, I began to get somewhat irritated I guess you would say because I had to get up a little earlier to take her, and sometimes I would have to wait on her, and it made me late to work. I really *enjoyed* our drive time though because we *did* talk about God a lot. I just was being a bit selfish! I asked her if she had heard anything about her car, and she said that it was going to cost approximately $200 to get it fixed, and they did not have the money right now. I had the $200 to give her, but felt very strong in my spirit that I was not supposed to.

The second week, I'm asking God again, "May I please just give her the $200 so I can have my drive time back to myself?" Still heard no in my spirit. A few more days went by. "Now, God, *please?*" Still no. Then the third week on a Friday, I asked again, and this time the Lord said, "Yes, *today*."

I went by the bank on my way to pick her up that Friday and took out the $200. When she got in my car, she looked a little down. We drove in pretty much silence to work that day. I didn't feel like she was in the mood to talk.

As we got to the office parking lot, I looked at her and handed her the envelope with the money and let her know that the Lord prompted me to give her the money for her and her husband to get their car fixed. Her eyes got big, and we both began to cry. She proceeded to tell me that the night before her husband had got down on his knees and asked *God* to help them with the car. You see, God was waiting on that man's prayer and his trust in *God* to help them get the car fixed, and God had me "standing by" to answer that prayer. Had I given them the money at the beginning, God would not have gotten the glory!

Thought for the Day: If you have everything you need and have a friend in need, it is a great idea to help them. It can be even *greater* if you learn to pray about it first and follow the prompting of the Holy Spirit. God's timing is everything!

DAY 26

Be joyful in hope, patient in affliction, faithful in prayer.
—Romans 12:12

Praying for others is a constant need. Prayer *does* work. My family has seen it over and over. The evidence that our prayers can help another person brings such joy! We must be faithful in praying for others, and patient if we do not see results, which is hard, but need to remember, everything is always *God's* timing.

My daughter was dating a young man that decided to join the military. She was in college and was very worried for him when he left for boot camp. We talked about that the best thing that she could do to ease her worry would be to pray for him. She went *all out* and prayed for him daily and wrote him encouraging letters.

This young man wasn't sure if he totally believed in God, so part of my daughter's focus was on God opening his eyes to who God really is and for him to grow in his faith. She would send him scriptures and ask God to bless him and keep him safe.

My daughter was able to attend his boot camp graduation. She could tell something was different about him when she first saw him. Although he had just gone through intense military training, he had a new "softness" about him. He told her how much he appreciated all of the prayers and the letters, and that they actually helped him get through some of the really rough patches.

He told her the story about his last week of boot camp when his team had to go through some of the most intense survival training. They had to backpack up a very steep mountain while carrying a very heavy load. He was almost to the top and felt he could not go on any longer. He was in intense pain and told her that visions of her prayers kept him going.

He continued to climb the steep mountain then felt the intense pain again and collapsed to the ground. He said he saw visions of her praying again, and then at that very moment, he felt something under his hand buried in the dirt. He pulled it out, and *it was a cross!* He felt an overcoming power to finish, and he conquered the rest of that mountain!

Finding that cross in the ground was eye-opening for him, and he started to understand the power of God and the power of prayer! Praise God!

Thought for the Day: Never stop praying for others. When you feel worried, pray for them. When someone hurts you, pray for them. When someone doesn't believe, pray for them. *Be faithful in prayer.*

DAY 27

Do not be anxious about anything, but in every situation, by prayer
and petition, with thanksgiving, present your requests to God.
—Philippians 4:6

We all want what is best for our children, especially when it comes
to the "mate" that they choose to be with. There seems to always be
that "he or she is not good enough for my child" mentality. We really
need to try and stay out of our children's mate choices because it does
no good to "fight that fight" in the *flesh*. We *really* need to be praying
starting the day that they are born for *God* to bring the right person
as their mate.

My daughter was in a relationship that I was not real happy
about. He was not very nice to her and treated her more like a pos-
session. He would never take the time to have a conversation with
me or my husband and would not look us in the eye. We both did
real good not to say anything to our daughter, and we welcomed this
young man into our home with love.

Inside, it was bothering me though. I did not like my daughter
being treated like that. I would pray and pray and pray. Then one
late summer evening, the Lord pressed upon my heart to pray for the
situation *at that very moment*. I went out by the pool and cried out to
God and asked Him to let *her* see who this young man really is, and
that he is not a very nice person. I felt the Holy Spirit on me and just
cried out to God for about fifteen minutes.

When I came into the house, my son saw my tear-stained face
and asked me what was wrong. I told him I had been outside crying

out to the Lord regarding his sister's current relationship. And then, about that time, my phone rang. It was my daughter. She was at the boyfriend's house, and she said, "Mommy, I am coming home. Will you please stay up so that I can talk to you?"

She got home and fell into my arms in tears. She told me that she didn't think she could be with this young man anymore. She said that about an hour earlier, as she was looking at him, this overwhelming feeling came over her, and she saw that he was unkind and felt in her heart that he was definitely not the one.

Praise God! We need to take *every* situation to God and pray about it. There is really nothing in our flesh that we could say or do that would make our loved ones change their mind about their mate choice—it usually just makes it worse. It is hard on parents, but you have to remember that the enemy is always trying to cause division in families, and mate choice is the target a lot of times. Give it to God and *trust* Him to work it out.

Thought for the Day: When you find yourself starting to worry about, or put down your friend or family's mate choice, close your mouth and *just pray*.

DAY 28

Therefore, my brothers and sisters, be eager to
prophesy, and do not forbid speaking in tongues.
—1 Corinthians 14:39

I talked about the importance of prophecy earlier in the book, and now comes another what I would call "controversial" subject from the Bible—speaking in tongues. I have to admit, I thought it sounded quite ludicrous and thought again that this must have only happened during the biblical times.

My first encounter with ever hearing about speaking in tongues was with the woman I spoke about earlier in the book who prophesied to me for the first time. She told me that I was going to be "baptized with the Holy Spirit" and that I would speak in tongues. I am sure I looked at her like she had two heads!

The very next day, a friend of mine dropped by and said she had been at a church meeting at her Catholic Church and received a brochure titled "What Does It Mean to Be Baptized with the Holy Spirit," and she felt led to bring it to me! (I can't make this stuff up—this truly happened!) I read the brochure, and my eyes were opened more about what it meant, and I began to pray about it and asked God to show me if I am supposed to get this "baptism."

A couple of weeks later, the "prophecy" friend invited me to go to a Pentecostal women's retreat. I heard "tongue talking" there for the first time in my life and was a little freaked out at first! Ha-ha! Then a lady next to me "fell out in the spirit," and I thought we needed to call 911! My friend was like, "No, the Holy Spirit is imparting something to her." Ummm, okay. Ha-ha!

The funny thing was, I was not in the least bit scared. I was actually "drawn" to these gifts of the spirit that I was learning about, and I wanted to know *more*. I felt at peace and like I was where God wanted me. I saw women coming together to pray and do things for the body of Christ such as healings and deliverances and prophecy to build each other up. It was awesome, and I knew I wanted to be a part of this work of God.

Then, a few weeks after the tongue-talking retreat, my friend invited me to a *revival*—the only revivals I knew about were those I saw on TV that looked pretty hokeypokey. Ha! I went to the revival with my friend, and boy, am I glad that I did! There was an awesome speaker, and guess what he was talking about?! The *baptism with the Holy Spirit*—I was praying to God to receive it.

The next thing I knew, the man was standing in front of me, laid his hand on my forehead, and said, "No more *fear*!" Then something that felt kind of "warm and goose bumpy" came over me, and my mouth was moving up and down kind of like I had the chills. I began to utter syllables that sounded like when those other people were speaking in tongues! I really still to this day do not really understand it, but I have faith that I received the baptism of the Holy Spirit. I do not have the "gift" of tongues, but I often pray in tongues when I do not know what to pray.

This subject is still something that I need to study further. I believe a change happened to me that day that definitely increased my faith. I know that I have definitely seen results after I've prayed in tongues. The Lord has awakened me in the middle of the night and has shown me a face, but it is unclear what I should pray for that person, so I will just utter my prayer language. I then find out later that the particular person had been going through something. I have to trust that God knew, and He used my vessel to send prayers to heaven.

Thought for the Day: Do not discount speaking in tongues. It is real, it is in the Bible. There is a difference between having the gift of speaking in tongues and giving a message that needs interpretation, than praying in tongues. I would encourage you to read more about what the Bible has to say about tongues.

DAY 29

For our struggle is not against flesh and blood, but against the
rulers, against the authorities, against the powers of this dark world
and against the spiritual forces of evil in the heavenly realms
—Ephesians 6:12–13

I used to hear this scripture and not really understand what it meant. I came to learn that the "authorities and powers of the dark world" are Satan's army, and they have their own heavenly realm and are constantly trying to keep God's people from knowing who they are in Christ. They are constantly at work to *bring us down*, and we *must* be aware of this spiritual battle. God has given us authority over this evil, but we have to understand how to fight that battle.

Knowing Jesus Christ as your Lord and Savior and getting the scriptures embedded in your heart and *praying* is key. The enemy *flees in terror* when God's Word is spoken. That is power right there! God has made sure that the enemy can be under our feet, but he's only under our feet if we are walking in the spirit and being obedient with how God says to win the battle—it's *not* a battle of flesh and blood.

I am about to tell you a story of how I fought and won against a demonic force that was trying to take down my daughter and her roommates. It may sound hokey, but it's the truth. It may sound like scary movie stuff, but when you know who you are in Christ and the authority you have been given and you are led by the Holy Spirit, it's *not* scary.

My mom and I were visiting my daughter her senior year at college in the house she and her two roommates lived in. All three of them had been battling illness after illness. We were there to try and bring some cheer and *fun*. The first night I was there, I was awakened in the middle of the night feeling like I was being choked! I sat straight up in bed and got out the name *Jesus*, and it went away.

The next morning when I woke up, I was thinking about what had happened to me, and I prayed, "What was *that*, God?" I heard in my spirit that there was a spirit of infirmity in that house, and I needed to cast it out! By this time, I had been in many church meetings where demonic forces had been cast out, so I was familiar with what needed to be done.

I told my daughter about it, and she said, "Let's do it." We joined hands and prayed for the spirit of infirmity to leave that house in the name of Jesus! As we prayed, we both had goosebumps from head to toe, and we knew God was with us.

My daughter asked me not to tell her roommates about the incident because it might "scare them." They were very involved in the church there, but this type of spiritual battle was not being taught at the church they attended. My daughter had been with me to church meetings before where it was taught though and knew about these things.

The roommates met up with us a little while later, and we began to talk about God. That was often a subject when I went to visit. They were all hungry for more of God. I happened to say something about angels all around us, and one of my daughter's roommates blurted out, "There is a *bad* spirit that comes in my room, Mrs. Tammy, and I 'see' it! It's a black shadowy figure!" *Wait, what did she just say?!* My daughter and I were shocked—her roommate had been actually seeing this spirit of infirmity and was afraid to tell my daughter about it! (You cannot make this stuff up!)

We told the roommate what had happened to me the night before, and that we cast that spirit of infirmity out of their house! There were many tears and hugs and praise to God! And those kids did *not* get sick again the rest of the schoolyear.

Thought for the Day: We have the power of God in us to *stop* evil forces. We need to stay prayed up and in the Word to know how to fight them properly. Listen for the Holy Spirit's promptings always, always before ever trying to cast out bad spirits. It is always all about *God's* timing and *not* our own.

DAY 30

But he said to me, "My grace is sufficient for you, for my power
is made perfect in weakness." Therefore I will boast all the more
gladly about my weaknesses, so that Christ's power may rest on me.
—2 Corinthians 12:9

Let's talk about a lighter subject than the demons we spoke about
in yesterday's devotional—*grace!* :-) I say "lighter" subject, but *grace*
is one of the most *important* subjects because it is the greatest gift
we could have ever been given—receiving eternal life through Jesus
Christ without ever having to *earn* it. Think about that—*eternal bliss
given to us* without our having to prove being worthy of it.

When I really began to understand the gift of *grace*, the way I
looked at trials, problems, and pains changed significantly. I understood in 2 Corinthians why God told Paul that He was not going
to remove the thorn in his side, and that what he had already been
given (*grace*) far outweighed anything that Paul may have to go
through while living temporarily on earth in the flesh. Plus, when
Paul thought about this weakness, it made him always turn to *God*
and that is what God wants—total trust and dependence on Him.
Letting *His* power and might rest on us for *God* to get the glory!

It's *so hard* though when we go through trials, problems, and
pains, but those are inevitable while we are in these fleshly bodies
on earth. And remember, the enemy is constantly trying to get our
eyes off of Jesus and grace, and when we do take our eyes off this, we
actually work to open *ourselves* up to a lot of the trials, problems, and
pains with our choices.

Oh, but His word promises, when we are *weak, He is strong*! We must turn to Him in prayer through these trials. Sometimes we may get to "see" why we had to go through them such as God was trying to work a certain behavior out of us or direct our path in a different way than we were trying to go in the flesh. Sometimes though we may never know the reason for the trials until we come face to face with Him in heaven. We just have to *trust*.

I have a "weakness" in my life that has caused me a great deal of pain over the years. I have asked God to remove it over and over. I finally understood the gift of *grace* though, and it led me to finally say to God not too long ago, "If this is the way it has to be until my last day on earth, God, then I'm okay because your *grace is enough*."

There is nothing I could ever go through in this temporary life on earth that could even compare to living an eternal life in heaven with my Heavenly Father where there will be *no more* tears, *no more* pain, *no more* fears. Hallelujah!

Thought for the Day: When you are going through a trial, *pray*. Ask God to show you if there is something you said or maybe did that opened up the door to it. *Thank Him always for the grace*—it truly is enough.

DAY 31

You, dear children, are from God and have overcome them, because
the one who is in you is greater than the one who is in the world.
—1 John 4:4

The Holy Spirit is *in* us, and the Bible tells us over and over that
the *battle against the devil* is already won; however, God's people tend
to forget this over and over. Why do they forget it? Because it's the
devil's job to constantly make us forget who we are in Christ by putting thoughts in our head, by putting obstacles and people in our
way, and to cause division and to cause us not to portray the character of God!

These thoughts from the devil must be recognized, captured,
and cast down! Greater is He that is in you, and *that* is the voice you
need to be listening to. The Holy Spirit is never going to have you
do or say anything that is outside the Word of God. That is how we
must "test" those thoughts.

The Holy Spirit gives us the power to *overcome* in every situation. What does that look like? Well, when a person's behavior
toward you is rude, and the thought in your head is *I must retaliate
with anger or bitterness*, then you capture that thought right then,
knowing anger and retaliation does *not* line up with the Word of
God, and you instead let the *Holy Spirit* rise up in you and respond
with *love*.

When you are in total disagreement about a friend's political
views and you want to respond and tell them how stupid they are—
allow the Holy Spirit to rise up in you and *not* respond with mean-

ness, and instead *pray* for your friend and for God to reveal *His* plan for politics.

There are so many *daily* opportunities to respond God's way, which will not lead to division or open the door for the enemy to get in.

When you are in traffic, the Holy Spirit can give you the power to overcome that driver that cut you off. In the grocery store, the Holy Spirit can give you the power to be patient and let the lady with all of the comparison coupons not make you angry. When you are at work and are not being recognized for doing outstanding work, the Holy Spirit can give you the power to understand that your treasures are being stored in heaven for working as unto the Lord and not fall into self-pity. If you want to go on a shopping spree, but doing so would put you in debt, the Holy Spirit can give you the power to choose not to go shopping!

I know those examples seem like minor scenarios for the Holy Spirit to help you overcome and respond like Jesus would—but *all* of these types of scenarios are being seen by God and are building up your Spirit man for you to overcome *all* of the devil's tactics. This is where the devil works hardest through us—if he can get us to act outside of *God's* character in the day-to-day activities and relationships, he's winning! A lot of Christians do not understand this, and that is why not many people in the world are attracted to Jesus. When we do not respond in everyday life situations with the character of God, we are not any help to God to build His Kingdom.

Thought for the Day: Understand who you are in Christ, and that the Holy Spirit is within you to help you overcome in *all* situations where the devil is trying to bring division. *Greater is he that is within you.*

DAY 32

For if you forgive other people when they sin against
you, your heavenly Father will also forgive you.
—Matthew 6:14

The Bible has *a lot* to say about *forgiveness*. Jesus told Peter in the book of Matthew to forgive "seventy times seven," and in the same book, God said He will not forgive us if we do not forgive others—*yikes*. Big motivation right there to forgive!

One of the most powerful scriptures about forgiving that made a huge impact on me was the parable of the unmerciful servant in Matthew chapter 18. The parable ended with the person who did not forgive being handed over to be put in a place of *torment*! Then scripture says that this is what God will do to a person who does not forgive!

Think about that—God will hand you over to be tormented in a state of "prison" here on earth if you do not *forgive*! That is powerful and sounds very scary! God will allow the enemy to torment you in your state of unforgiveness—not a place I ever want to be!

I have been in numerous situations where I have had to forgive when it's been very difficult. I wanted the person punished for what they had done! I would fall into such self-pity. Poor, pitiful me. How could you allow this, God? I want you to pay them back, God. My thoughts were all wrong.

God had to show me just how wrong my thinking was by Jesus's example after being captured, abused, and crucified. Jesus said while hanging on the cross when he was about to *die*, "Father, forgive them for they know not what they do." Wow—it showed me how the people who have hurt me also probably do not know what they were doing!

It is God's desire for everyone to get an understanding of who they are in Christ and have an opportunity to receive that *grace*. The people who do not know Him act out and do things that are led by the spirit of the world—the devil. God wants us to look at them through *His* eyes and *pray* for them and hope to be an influence on them to come into His Kingdom. This great commission God has for us to "go and make disciples" cannot be met if we just hold their actions against them.

As hard as it sounds, we must ask God to forgive them, and we must forgive them. Otherwise, you will be held here on earth in that state of being tormented, and you will not have any *peace*. Think about *that*. Why would you want to remain in a place of torment?

Forgiveness does *not* mean "forgetting" or dismissing what the person has done. It means getting *yourself* to a place of *peace*.

Thought of the Day: Sometimes it is through deep tears of pain that we have to forgive, but we *must* do it in order to live in *peace* and get out of a place of torment.

DAY 33

Yet for us there is but one God, the Father, from whom all things
came and for whom we live; and there is but one Lord, Jesus
Christ, through whom all things came and through whom we live.
—1 Corinthians 8:6

Here we are on the last day of this devotional journey. I pray that I
have inspired you to make Jesus the *Lord* of your life. We were made
for God, by God, and there is really nothing else to aim for but the
will of God for your life!

The beautiful news is that He knows we are human, and we
make mistakes. He knows that the enemy is going to try *everything* he
can to get us over to his camp, but *greater is He that is in us*! Let the
Holy Spirit help you to *overcome* and stand victorious in the battle
that was already won!

We must fill our lives with constant communication with our
maker to stay on course and not get tricked by the enemy! We must
get the Word written on our hearts to help in that battle—it is a
spiritual battle. We are not "of" this world, we are just in it for a
temporary time.

I have learned that by looking at all things in life through *God's*
eyes, I can experience *love, joy, and peace*. Everything He does has a
purpose, and He will work *all things* together for our good because
we love Him and are called according to *His* purpose. Making anything else the Lord of your life on earth will just bring heartache and
destruction.

Remember that He said, "Narrow is the way, and not many people will find it." Be one of the ones who *finds* it! *Stop, pray, listen, obey.* It takes practice, but eventually you will learn to live *supernaturally* naturally.

Much love, blessings and favor to you! Tammy.

About the Author

Tammy McKie is a lover of God's Word, a teacher of God's truth, a reflector of God's love, and an encourager to those around her. For the past twenty-five years, she has served as Sunday school coordinator, teacher, and youth leader. She has led Bible studies, ministered at outreaches, spoken at conferences, led prayer services, and has held weekly church services at a mental health facility.

She has a passion to reach those who may never step foot in a church by showing them the love of God and helping them understand who they are created to be, and that being a Christian means following Christ in everyday life and not just attending a church service once a week. She wants to be a source of inspiration everywhere she goes and teach the importance of listening to the voice of the Holy Spirit.

CPSIA information can be obtained
at www.ICGtesting.com
Printed in the USA
JSHW022348160919
1499JS00001B/3